The Mysterious & Unknown

ESP

Other titles in *The Mysterious & Unknown* series:

The Mysterious  & Unknown

ESP

by Stuart A. Kallen

ReferencePoint Press®

San Diego, CA

©2013 ReferencePoint Press, Inc.
Printed in the United States

For more information, contact:
ReferencePoint Press, Inc.
PO Box 27779
San Diego, CA 92198
www.ReferencePointPress.com

LIBRARY OF CONGRESS CATALOGING-IN-PUBLICATION DATA

Kallen, Stuart A., 1955–
   ESP / by Stuart A. Kallen.
      p. cm. -- (Mysterious & unknown)
   Includes bibliographical references and index.
   ISBN 978-1-60152-472-0 (hardback) -- ISBN 1-60152-472-2 (hardback)1. Extrasensory perception. I. Title.
   BF1321.K35   2013
   133.8--dc23

                                                                                      2012011478

CONTENTS

FOREWORD

"Strange is our situation here upon earth."
—*Albert Einstein*

Since the beginning of recorded history, people have been perplexed, fascinated, and even terrified by events that defy explanation. While science has demystified many of these events, such as volcanic eruptions and lunar eclipses, some remain outside the scope of the provable. Do UFOs exist? Are people abducted by aliens? Can some people see into the future? These questions and many more continue to puzzle, intrigue, and confound despite the enormous advances of modern science and technology.

It is these questions, phenomena, and oddities that Reference-Point Press's *The Mysterious & Unknown* series is committed to exploring. Each volume examines historical and anecdotal evidence as well as the most recent theories surrounding the topic in debate. Fascinating primary source quotes from scientists, experts, and eyewitnesses as well as in-depth sidebars further inform the text. Full-color illustrations and photos add to each book's visual appeal. Finally, source notes, a bibliography, and a thorough index provide further reference and research support. Whether for research or the curious reader, *The Mysterious & Unknown* series is certain to satisfy those fascinated by the unexplained.

INTRODUCTION

Senses in Another Reality

Within hours of the 9/11 terrorist attacks in New York City, Washington, DC, and Pennsylvania, government agencies launched a massive manhunt for the mastermind behind the assault. The Federal Bureau of Investigation (FBI) put Osama bin Laden at the top of its Ten Most Wanted Fugitives and Most Wanted Terrorists lists. The US government offered a $25 million reward for his capture. However, agents working for military and intelligence agencies in the United States and Europe could not locate the terrorist mastermind.

While military forces searched for Bin Laden with soldiers on the ground, high-tech spy planes, and satellite imaging, the British Ministry of Defence tried a less conventional approach. In a top secret mission, the Ministry of Defence recruited 12 psychics to locate Bin Laden's secret lair. According to documents declassified in 2007, the psychics practiced something called remote viewing (RV), a technique associated with extrasensory perception (ESP). Those who believe in remote viewing say that

7

a psychic can go into a trancelike state and envision details of events at a distant location.

Before the psychics were used to find Bin Laden, the Ministry of Defence attempted to test their remote viewing skills. The psychics were blindfolded and asked to identify the contents of sealed envelopes which contained photographs of public figures and everyday objects such as a knife. About one in four succeeded; the others, including one psychic who fell asleep during

The hunt for Osama bin Laden, the mastermind behind the 9/11 terrorist attacks, was conducted with the help of spy planes and satellite imaging—and a dozen psychics. British authorities asked the psychics to use an ESP technique in which they envision details of distant events while in a trancelike state.

the exercise, failed. Those who succeeded were asked to focus their remote viewing skills on maps and photographs of regions where Bin Laden was believed to be hiding.

Great Britain's remote viewing psychic experiment, probably conducted in 2002, was discontinued after a short time. Bin Laden was finally tracked down in Abbottabad, Pakistan, in 2011, most likely by spies working for the US government. He was killed in his compound by a unit of US Navy SEALS.

Whether psychics played any part in the final Bin Laden drama is unknown. However, reports declassified in 1995 show that the United States also has a history of using psychics. According to those reports, 16 remote viewers worked for the Central Intelligence Agency (CIA) between the early 1970s and the mid-1990s. The CIA hoped that remote viewing would help the agency find weapons caches, terrorists, and secret military installations. The CIA purportedly shut down the program in 1995. However, investigative reporter Gus Russo wrote in 2007 that the RV program was not discontinued but was transferred to the National Security Agency (NSA). The NSA has denied such a program exists, but Russo and others believe remote viewing has been used as one tool in the war on terror in recent years.

The Sixth Sense

Remote viewing is one of several ESP techniques. Others include clairvoyance, telepathy, and precognition. *Clairvoyance* is French for "clear vision." Those who practice clairvoyance use their mental powers to gather hidden information about people, objects, and events in the physical world. Those who practice telepathy claim to "read" peoples' minds, thoughts, and emotions. Precognition, or future sight, involves looking into the future and describing events that have not yet happened.

Because extrasensory perception is different from the five physical senses—sight, hearing, smell, taste, and touch—ESP is known as a "sixth sense." Those who practice ESP sometimes refer to the information they glean as a gut instinct, premonition, or hunch. No matter what it is called, believers think ESP originates in a second, or alternate, reality.

Common Experiences

Extrasensory perception is often a subject of controversy. Skeptics do not believe ESP is any more real than ghosts, vampires, or UFOs. Several organizations, including the Committee for Skeptical Inquiry (CSI) and the James Randi Educational Foundation (JREF), work to discourage belief in ESP and other paranormal phenomena. Among scientists in the National Academy of Sciences, 96 percent say they are skeptical that ESP exists.

Belief in ESP is much stronger among the general public. Polls repeatedly show that about half of all Americans believe in ESP. Perhaps this is because extrasensory occurrences are common in everyday life. For example, many people have found themselves thinking about a friend or relative only to have that person call on the phone moments later. Others have had dreams about future events or sensed that a relative was sick or dying. These events are often defined as coincidental, but believers say such experiences are related to ESP.

Formal Research

The belief in ESP is as old as human history. Rulers in ancient Greece often consulted clairvoyants and oracles. In the Bible prophets read minds, predicted the future, and described events taking place at a great distance.

In the twentieth century, researchers and scientists worked diligently to prove the existence of ESP. By the 1930s, laboratory and field research concerning telepathy, precognition, clairvoyance, and RV was being conducted at Stanford University in California, Duke University in North Carolina, and several private and governmental institutions. In the twenty-first century, ESP research has been conducted at universities in Arizona and Virginia as well as 150 different institutions located in 30 countries.

Although researchers continue to experiment with ESP, no one has proved that any truth lies behind claims of ESP abilities. Scientific proof aside, hunches and premonitions are part of daily life for many. As long as believers continue to assert that the sixth sense exists, extrasensory perception will remain a subject of controversy and fascination.

CHAPTER 1

Investigating ESP

The renowned American author Mark Twain was a firm believer in extrasensory perception. In an 1891 article in *Harper's* magazine Twain describes an event that provided a basis for his belief. He says that he had an idea for a book called *The Great Bonanza* in 1889. The story would be about the Nevada silver mining boom, in which thousands of people rushed to the state to strike it rich digging for silver. Twain did not want to write *The Great Bonanza* himself—he thought the project would be perfect for an author friend of his named William H. Wright who lived in Nevada. Although he had not seen Wright in 10 years and did not even know if he was alive or dead, Twain drafted a long, detailed book outline to send to him. However, Twain did not get around to mailing it—he put it aside on a shelf by his desk. Seven days later a large envelope was delivered to Twain's home in Connecticut, and he knew what it was before he broke the seal. In order to amaze a visiting relative, Twain offered to perform an act of extrasensory perception:

Now I will do a miracle. I will tell you everything this letter contains. . . . Mr. Wright proposes to make a book about the silver mines and the Great Bonanza, and asks what I, as a friend, think of the idea. He says his subjects are to be so and so, their order and sequence so and so, and he will close with a history of the chief feature of the book, the *Great Bonanza*.[1]

Twain opened the envelope and showed it to his relative. He had been completely accurate. Wright's letter contained exactly what Twain predicted. In addition, the letter was written in Nevada on the same date that Twain had written his letter in Connecticut. Twain continues:

Wright's letter and the one which I had written to him but never sent were in substance the same. Necessarily this could not have come by accident; such elaborate accidents cannot happen. . . . I could not doubt—there was not tenable reason for doubting—that Mr. Wright's mind and mine had been in close and crystal-clear communication with each other across three thousand miles of mountain and desert. I did not consider that both minds *originated* the succession of ideas, but that one mind originated them and simply telegraphed them to the other.[2]

Twain determined that Wright had the idea for *Great Bonanza* first and had mentally transferred detailed thoughts about the book to Twain. Twain labeled this and similar events "mental telegraphy."

Distant Experiences

At the time Twain wrote this article, extrasensory perception was a matter of intense interest in the United States and Great Britain. Dozens of books and hundreds of articles about ESP were published in the 1880s and 1890s. In addition, several scholarly institutions had been established to study ESP-related phenomena. This occurred at a time when millions of people in the United States and Europe had taken an interest in spiritualism. Spiritualists believe in paranormal phenomena, unusual experiences that defy scientific explanation, such as spirit communication, telepathy, and premonitions about the future.

The spiritualist movement, as some called it, was launched in 1848 when sisters Maggie Fox, age 11, and Kate Fox, age 14, reported weird rapping and crackling within the walls of their small home in Arcadia, New York. The sisters claimed the noises were "spirit raps," a form of code used by a supernatural entity the girls called Mr. Splitfoot.

Descriptions of the spirit raps by Mr. Splitfoot were reported in the national press. Soon after, hundreds of people flocked to the Fox home to hear the unearthly spirit communications. Within two years a sort of spirit mania swept across the United States. Countless people took advantage of the spiritualism fad and went into business as mediums—spirit messengers who claimed they could communicate with ghosts, angels, or other cosmic spirits. By the 1870s, about 1.5 million people claimed to be spiritualists in the United States.

Research Without Prejudice

Early spiritualists were mostly interested in communicating with the dead. However, there was also a growing fascination with other ESP-related phenomena. These included reading minds, pre-

dicting the future, and seeing events otherwise hidden from view.

By the 1880s spiritualism was as popular in Great Britain as in the United States. In London the movement attracted the attention of poet, philosopher, and scholar Frederic W.H. Myers, who founded the Society for Psychical Research (SPR) in 1882. Myers believed that some spiritualist claims might be authentic, but he also knew that many so-called mediums made false claims about their ESP skills. These swindlers often charged lonely widows large sums to contact their dead husbands or children.

Myers established the SPR in an effort to ferret out fraud. As Myers wrote in thick Victorian prose, he wanted to study ESP and ghostly hauntings "without prejudice or prepossession of any kind, and in the same spirit of exact and unimpassioned enquiry which has enabled science to solve so many problems, once not less obscure or less hotly debated."[3]

No one had ever studied ESP in a rigorous manner, and the prospect of doing so attracted some of Britain's most respected thinkers. They included philosopher and economist Henry Sidgwick, physicist William Fletcher Barrett, and classical scholar Edmund Gurney. These men had already accepted the general theory that the sixth sense, extrasensory perception, truly existed in human beings. They wanted to find out how ESP worked, put forth possible causes for it, and learn to reproduce it in controlled conditions. In order to do so, members of the SPR devised various tests and experiments. They also created mathematical formulas that could identify the odds of a particular ESP experience occurring by chance.

The investigators decided that they needed to document as many cases of verifiable ESP as they could find, and they were dogged in their pursuit. In 1883 alone they sent out over 10,000 letters to clairvoyants, psychics, and fortune-tellers who claimed

A Zener deck
consists of 25 cards
with five repeated
patterns—a circle,
a square, a cross,
three wavy lines
(called waves),
and a star.

to possess the sixth sense. At the same time, newspaper reports about the society inspired thousands of average citizens to write letters detailing their experiences with ESP. Members of the SPR interviewed promising subjects in a thorough, scholarly manner. Researchers had to confront several problems during each inquiry, as author and psychic researcher Rosalind Heywood explains:

> There is a very human desire for the marvelous and an equally human desire to feel important. Quite unconsciously, therefore, some people will twist evidence [of ESP] to sound watertight when there are tiny leaks in it. Others . . . may have a latent tendency to hysteria, resulting in hallucinations which seem to them to have an exterior origin when in fact they are self-created.[4]

Two Types of Telepathy

Members of the SPR collected a large body of seemingly real ESP experiences. Much of the researchers' focus centered on what was then called thought transference. Like Twain's experience with his writer friend, this occurs when one person seems able to send thoughts to or receive thoughts from another person, oftentimes at a great distance. Myers coined a word for this phenomenon, telepathy, from the Greek words *tele*, or "distant," and *pathe*, meaning "experience." Myers defined telepathy as "all cases of impression received at a distance without the normal operation of recognized sense organs."[5]

The SPR investigators believed telepathy occurred in two different ways. Sometimes the telepath and a subject, called an agent, actively worked together. The agent concentrated on a

Members of the Society for Psychical Research began documenting ESP experiences in the late 1800s. As part of their research they contacted thousands of clairvoyants, fortune-tellers, palm readers, and others in hopes of hearing detailed accounts of their ESP-related experiences.

word or object, and the telepath "read" his or her thoughts. Other times, telepathy happened spontaneously; that is, unprompted or accidentally. In such cases the telepath would be struck suddenly by mental pictures or words from an agent who was unaware of sending the thoughts. Researchers found spontaneous telepathy most often occurred during times of crises when a sick or dying person sent a mental call for help to a relative, friend, or member of the same household.

Card Guessing

The SPR formed the Thought-Transference Committee to conduct experiments with those who claimed to actively practice nonspontaneous ESP. The first subjects to be studied were the four teenage daughters of the Reverend Andrew Macreight Creery. In a letter to the SPR, Reverend Creery claimed that each of his daughters was blessed with incredible powers. He said he tested them, and they were able to read an agent's mind and identify thoughts about objects in a room, names of people, and lines of poems. On one occasion, he commented, they were also able to successfully name 17 playing cards in a row, which were randomly pulled from a deck. According to Creery, "When the children were in good humour, and excited by the wonderful nature of their successful guessing, they very seldom made a mistake. . . . We soon found that a great deal depended on the steadiness with which the ideas were kept in the minds of 'the thinkers,' and upon the energy with which they

"When the children were in good humour, and excited by the wonderful nature of their successful guessing, they very seldom made a mistake."
— The Reverend Andrew Macreight Creery.

Studying Inner Space

Apollo 14 astronaut Edgar Dean Mitchell, who conducted telepathy experiments during his moon landing mission, said he felt ecstasy and bliss looking out the window of his space module as it hurtled through space. He described feeling a connection with the universe, an experience he compared to a religious revelation. As a 1974 article in *People* magazine explains, the moon mission changed Mitchell's life:

> After between 25 and 30 hours of such mystic perceptions, Mitchell came back to earth determined to do something about the truth he understood so starkly from a lunar distance. The solution, he felt, lay in a sort of planet-wide consciousness-raising, which would be accomplished through the scientific applications of parapsychology (sometimes called psi) . . . ESP, clairvoyance, telepathy and psychokinesis (the use of psychic energy to bring about physical changes, like bending forks with well aimed thinking). All these and more could be employed in the quest for greater realization of the power of the human mind.

People, "Edgar Mitchell's Strange Voyage," 1974. www.people.com.

willed the ideas to pass."[6] Creery also claimed that the telepathic powers were not limited to his own family. Experiments with the neighbor's children also yielded similar results.

In 1882 Barrett led a 10-day study of the girls together and individually. They were asked to identify hidden items or playing cards. In one test Mary Creery, aged 17, correctly identified a white penknife and a box of almonds but failed to guess the identity of a box of chocolates and a coin. During card-guessing experiments all four sisters seemed remarkably adept at telepathy. For an average person the odds are 1 in 51 of correctly guessing a single card in a 52-card deck. During 382 tests on the four sisters, the girls correctly identified cards 202 times. On several occasions individual Creery sisters were able to correctly name five cards in a row. Barrett said the odds of this happening by chance were "over 142 million to one."[7]

A Sudden Heart Attack

While members of the Thought-Transference Committee studied card guessing, other SPR members looked into spontaneous telepathy. As with the Creery sisters, the researchers selected subjects based on letters sent to the organization. A typical case was described by a woman identified as Mrs. Bettany. Her spontaneous ESP was a case of telepathy initiated by a crisis.

Bettany claimed that when she was 10 years old she was heading home from school, reading a geometry book as she walked along a country lane. She was suddenly struck by a strong image of her parents' bedroom, known among family members as the White Room. Bettany saw her mother lying on the floor, seemingly dead. The girl was puzzled by this vision since her mother appeared to be in perfect health when she left home that morning. Bettany picks up the story:

The vision must have remained some minutes, during which time my real surroundings appeared to pale and die out; but as the vision faded, actual surroundings came back, at first dimly, and then clearly. I could not doubt that what I had seen was real, so, instead of going home, I went at once to the house of our medical man and found him at home. . . . I led the doctor straight to the White Room, where we found my mother actually lying as in my vision. This was true even to minute details. She had been seized suddenly by an attack at the heart, and would soon have breathed her last but for the doctor's timely advent.[8]

Zener Cards

While Bettany's father verified the story, her mother and the doctor were long dead by the time the account was brought to the attention of researchers. Like many reports of spontaneous telepathy, Bettany's incident of crisis telepathy was difficult to prove and harder to analyze scientifically. As such, card guessing remained the most useful way to research telepathy since the statistical odds of correctly picking a playing card were easily understood. The mathematical formula for beating those odds was also well known. However, in 1930 Joseph Banks Rhine, a psychology professor at Duke University in North Carolina, found a problem with card guessing.

Rhine believed that a traditional pack of cards was useful to expert card guessers like the Cleery sisters, who already possessed ESP. With a talent for telepathy, experts could name both the card number and the suit (club, heart, spade, or diamond). Rhine wanted to study incidents of telepathy in the general population.

He believed it was too difficult for an average individual to guess two separate identifiers, the number and suit of a card. Rhine wanted a simpler method for testing ESP. He consulted with psychologist Karl E. Zener who had an answer to the problem. Zener created a smaller deck of cards for testing telepathy. That deck, which now bears his name, consists of 25 cards with five repeated patterns—a circle, a square, a cross, three wavy lines (called waves), and a star. With five symbols repeated five times within the deck of 25 cards, the odds that a person can correctly name the card by chance is one in five, or 20 percent.

A Radical Development for Science

Working with his wife and colleague, Louisa, Rhine founded the Parapsychology Laboratory at Duke to measure the presence of telepathy among the general public. (Rhine coined the term "parapsychology," later abbreviated as "psi," to replace the older phrase "psychical research.") While Louisa collected stories about spontaneous telepathy, Rhine conducted thousands of telepathy tests with student volunteers, using the Zener cards.

During a typical test, a researcher picked up a Zener card and concentrated on the symbol. The student attempted to name it. Rhine believed that average people experienced flashes of ESP and could often beat the 20 percent odds. Some students performed better than others, but one star subject, Hubert E. Pearce Jr., exhibited surprising results. During a series of 100 tests conducted in 1933, Pearce averaged 6 to 11 correct hits per run (24 to 44 percent).

Excited by the results, Rhine put Pearce through several thousand trials. The grueling experiments were designed to ensure that there could be no cheating. The researcher handling the cards was placed in one campus schoolroom while Pearce was located in a different building 300 feet (91m) away. The researcher synchronized his watch with Pearce's so the tests could proceed at the exact same time. The cards were selected at 1-minute intervals for a period of 25 minutes. The researcher did not even look at the cards but placed each one face down on the table while Pearce wrote down his impressions. Remarkably, during the first 12 tests, Pearce picked 119 of 300 cards correctly.

Pearce also scored zero at times (missing every card), but on one occasion he named the entire pack of 25 correctly. Rhine calculated the odds of achieving a 100 percent score by chance were one in a quadrillion. (A quadrillion is written with the number 10 followed by 15 zeros.) Rhine wrote about the experiment: "[We] were forced to decide that, whatever clairvoyance or the extrasensory perception of objects *is*, this was a case of it. It was a case in which results were obtained under the strictest control. . . . [Such] a demonstration was in itself a new and radical development for science."[9]

Rhine acknowledged the test did not explain what ESP was or how similar results could be reproduced. Nevertheless, when Rhine published his 1934 book *Extra-Sensory Perception*, he concluded that ESP was "an actual and demonstrable occurrence."[10]

Heated Controversy

Not everyone agreed with Rhine's assessment. His book generated heated controversy among psychologists and skeptics. Some questioned the complex mathematical formulas Rhine used to determine the odds of naming cards by chance. Others questioned Rhine's experimental methods, claiming he only reported on positive results and ignored failures. One critic noted that

Rhine thought some test subjects disliked him and were guessing wrong on purpose to spite him. Rhine admitted as much but felt that to put those scores in with the rest of his test data would be misleading.

While arguments raged over Rhine's methods, his book generated intense excitement in the press. Articles about Rhine's theories were widely covered in magazines and newspapers. This attention helped make the terms "ESP" and "extrasensory perception" household words.

Although Pearce was Rhine's star card guesser, he seems to have lost his ESP abilities after two years of testing, and his later scores fell below average. Parapsychologist Dean Radin explains this was common in many other high-scoring individuals: "The obvious reason for the declines is that the tests are exciting, fun, and motivating for about 10 minutes. . . . [Then the] test becomes more and more painfully boring until eventually you'd rather poke a stick in your eye than continue to guess cards."[11]

"In Telepathy Space Doesn't Matter"

Although he conducted 90,000 tests before publishing his book, Rhine was never bored by his quest to prove the existence of ESP. He continued his work at Duke for several decades and wrote many other books about ESP. Louisa also published several books that included some of the 7,000 cases she had collected concerning spontaneous psi. In 1965 the Rhines created the Foundation for Research on the Nature of Man (FRNM). The institute was renamed the Rhine Research Center in 1995 and continues to study ESP phenomena in the twenty-first century.

Rhine's work seldom generated headlines after the 1940s, but ESP became a subject of controversy once again in 1971. The *New York Times* reported that while Apollo 14 astronaut Edgar Dean

Mitchell was in outer space, he conducted a Zener symbol experiment with Rhine.

Apollo 14, launched January 31, 1971, was the fourth American mission to the moon. As part of the crew, Mitchell was the sixth person to walk on the lunar surface. The astronaut had been following Rhine's work for several years and believed in ESP. Mitchell was curious to know whether telepathy would work over a distance of 200,000 miles (321,868km). In order to find out, the astronaut secretly coordinated an experiment with Rhine, two NASA research physicists, and a Swedish psychic named Olof Jonsson who was living in Chicago at the time.

Because Mitchell could not take a deck of Zener cards into the zero gravity of outer space, he printed tables with the symbols on a few sheets of paper. During rest periods, while the Apollo 14 space capsule was hurtling through space, Mitchell concentrated on each individual symbol for about 15 seconds, sending his thought to four people. Six sessions were conducted during the course of the mission. The four subjects on earth made 200 guesses in total, and were correct 51 times. Working with Rhine, Mitchell concluded the odds of this occurring were one in 13,000. The astronaut believed the experiment was successful and proved the validity of ESP. Mitchell later told an interviewer:

> The question was whether the effect [telepathy] fell off with distance, and the answer is no. People had thought this, but no one had ever proved it at distances of hundreds of thousands of miles. Of course, one experiment doesn't make anything change, but it did show that what had worked in the laboratory also worked in space with the same very positive results. Professionals in the fields thought it was very significant. In telepathy, space doesn't matter.[12]

Ganzfeld Experiments

Even as Mitchell was conducting his outer space experiments, telepathy research was moving beyond simple Zener card tests. Researchers had determined that ESP seemed to be stronger in subjects who were relaxed, drifting to sleep, in a trance, or hypnotized. It seemed that when the five normal senses were not in use, as when a person was falling asleep, the sixth sense grew stronger. To test this theory Charles Honorton devised sensory deprivation experiments, testing for ESP when the five senses were not distracted by the surrounding environment.

Honorton placed his subjects, called receivers, in reclining chairs and lit the test room with red lights. Ping pong balls, which were cut in half, were placed over their eyes. The receivers wore

A test subject undergoes a ganzfeld telepathy experiment. The red light, ping pong balls on the eyes, and white noise played through headphones are supposed to create sensory deprivation and hallucinations to allow the flow of mental images from researchers to the test subjects.

headphones that played the sound of ocean waves breaking or a hissing static sound called white noise.

Honorton's sensory deprivation technique came to be called the *ganzfeld* effect, German for "entire field." Many people placed under ganzfeld conditions said they experienced a pleasant, dreamy state of awareness within a few minutes. After 15 minutes, receivers were asked to free-associate; that is, to say whatever popped into their minds.

As receivers free-associated, researchers in another room concentrated on photographs that were separated into four groups. The photo groups might include pictures of fish in the ocean, pictures of people engaged in various activities, or city and nature scenes. The researchers attempted to send mental images of specific pictures to the receivers. After the experiment ended, receivers were asked to guess which one of the four sets of photos the agents had targeted.

Between 1974 and 1981, Honorton conducted 42 ganzfeld experiments. The odds were one in four, or 25 percent, that a receiver would pick the correct set of photos. However, under ganzfeld conditions, the receivers achieved a success rate of 38 percent. According to Honorton, the odds of this happening by chance were less than one in a billion.

As with earlier ESP experiments, skeptics criticized the researcher's test methods and conclusions. Some believed that during follow-up interviews after the tests, the receivers were prompted to give correct answers. Others faulted the highly complex mathematical formulas Honorton used to figure the odds.

Computerized Tests

By the early 1990s, most psychologists were highly skeptical of psi phenomena. Annual surveys showed that only 34 percent of psychologists believed in ESP compared with 55 percent of college professors and 77 percent of academics in the arts, humanities, and education. These figures had changed little by 2011 when psychologist Daryl J. Bem published the results of a decade-long ESP experiment he had conducted at Cornell University in New York where he was a professor.

Bem devised a 20-minute computerized test in which two curtains appeared on a monitor. One curtain hid a photograph, the other covered a blank screen. The location of the photo was selected randomly by the computer. One thousand students were asked to take the test, which involved clicking the computer mouse on the curtain they believed covered the picture. While the odds are 50/50 that a subject would correctly pick the hidden photo, the overall score of the tests was a significant 53 percent. According to Bem, the new tests provided more evidence that ESP is real.

The results of Bem's tests were widely reported in the academic and popular press. However, according to the *New York Times*, some scientists believed Bem's conclusions were based on faulty research. According to psychology professor and skeptic Ray Hyman, "It's craziness, pure craziness. . . . I think it's just an embarrassment for the entire field [of psychology]."[13]

Defying Logic and Science

Hyman's comments show that more than 120 years after Mark Twain described his telepathic experiences in *Harpers*, the debate over ESP remains unsettled. Surveys continue to show that one-third of all psychologists say ESP is an absolute impossibility, a view that is held by only 2 percent of the general public.

Perhaps widespread belief in psi is a result of personal

experiences with spontaneous telepathy. While many gamblers go broke trying to guess the next card in a poker game, many people have had a premonition that someone is about to knock on the door or call moments before it happens. Such events defy scientific analysis and suggest that ESP will remain one of life's mysteries.

CHAPTER 2

Clairvoyance and the Senses

Long before the term "extrasensory perception" came into use in the 1930s, ESP was generally referred to as "clairvoyance." The term defines the psychic ability to mentally visualize distant or hidden images. Clairvoyance can be used to detect unseen objects, persons, locations, and events. Psychiatrist Diane Hennacy Powell calls clairvoyance "a psychic telescope, periscope, or camera."[14] Clairvoyants can aim their psychic cameras at the living, the dead, or even at people not yet born.

It might be said that clairvoyants integrate the sixth sense—extrasensory perception—to work with the five known senses. This allows clairvoyants to "see" a picture of an event in the mind, "hear" the voices of the dead, "feel" the emotions of a distant person, "taste" a substance without putting it in the mouth, and even "smell" a scent emitted by a spirit.

While these perceptions are all referred to as clairvoyance, each psychic sense has its own name. Hearing spirits is called clairaudience, feeling emotions or vibrations is clairsentience, clairvoyantly tasting is called clairgustance, and sniffing out paranormal matters is clairalience. Mediums may draw upon one or more of these psychic senses when practicing clairvoyance.

Clairvoyant Speaking and Writing

Some clairvoyants function while fully awake and conscious; others enter a hypnotic dreamlike trance and appear to be sleeping. For example, the psychic Edgar Cayce was first known as the Sleeping Prophet in the 1910s because he conducted clairvoyant readings while lying down, seemingly asleep. By contrast, some clairvoyants twitch, shake, swoon, yell, scream, or exhibit other shocking types of behavior.

Whatever the physical state of the medium, clairvoyance often involves channeling, or relaying messages, from the spirits. Clairvoyants channel in various ways. Some use what is called automatic writing, jotting down messages said to be from beyond the realm of the physical world. Oftentimes those engaged in automatic writing compose their works quickly and effortlessly, not thinking about the words or pictures they are putting on paper.

Clairvoyants who use their voices to channel spirit messages often perform what is called automatic speech. The medium may spontaneously speak using a normal tone of voice. However, the spirit voice might also be delivered as a deep grumble, a high-pitched squeak, or some other unusual tone. Words may be clear, inaudible, in a foreign tongue, or even in an unknown language.

The Martian Cycles

In the late 1890s the medium Hélène Smith engaged in both automatic writing and automatic speech. She contacted spirits and spoke and wrote in a language she claimed was from another planet. Smith, whose real name was Catherine-Elise Müller, was born in Hungary. In the early 1890s her séances attracted a large following in Switzerland. She was renowned for communicating with the French poet and playwright Victor Hugo, who had died in the previous decade.

Like most mediums, Smith worked with a spirit guide. Spiritualists believe spirit guides are a form of nonhuman energy that aid or escort mediums during séances. Smith's spirit guide was named Léopold, purportedly a reincarnation of the Count de Ca-

The medium Hélène Smith claimed she could travel to Mars (pictured) with the help of her spirit guide. Her travels were accomplished, she said, while in a trancelike state that enabled her to visit with and speak to the inhabitants of Mars.

gliostro. The count was not a member of the nobility but a medium whose real name was Joseph Balsamo. He was allegedly the lover of the eighteenth-century French queen Marie Antoinette.

By the mid-1890s Smith had moved beyond channeling dead poets. She claimed that, with the help of her spirit guide Léopold, she began traveling to Mars while in a trance state called the Martian Cycles. When Smith entered a Martian Cycle, Léopold took control of her body. The medium's initial calm sleep gave way to loud sighs, agitation, jerky muscular contractions, and rhythmic movements of the head and hands. While in this state, Smith began touring Mars and speaking to Martians, translating the words into French as she did so. Smith described Mars as a place populated by humanoids that flew in aircraft and traveled across the terrain in self-powered vehicles. Doglike creatures with heads resembling cabbages fetched objects for their owners and also took dictation, writing down spoken words.

During the Martian Cycles Smith engaged in automatic writing with a quivering hand, jotting down shaky symbols. Each symbol represented an individual Martian. They had names such as Traveler, Runner, Guide, Town Crier, Dog Breeder, Virgin Girl, Hole Digger, Bearer of Sacred Water, Guardian, and Fiancé.

Playing to the Audience

The Martian Cycles continued for several years before Smith began visiting another planet she called Ultra-Mars. The Ultra-Martians were grotesque troll-like creatures. They were 3 feet (0.9m) tall, but their heads were 6 feet (1.8m) wide. The Ultra-Martians lived in cabins 10 feet (3m) below the surface, accessible only though tunnels. The Ultra-Martian language had a different rhythm and slower pace than the Martian spoken by Smith during earlier trances.

Edgar Cayce: The Sleeping Prophet

Edgar Cayce was one of the most influential clairvoyants of the twentieth century and was an international celebrity between 1910 and 1945. Cayce, a high school dropout, began his career as a clairvoyant healer. He claimed to be able to diagnose illness in patients who wrote him letters or called him on the phone. He did so in a sleeplike trance that earned him the nickname the Sleeping Prophet.

During the 1920s Cayce moved beyond healing and began describing travels to exotic locations during his trance sessions. He claimed to visit ancient Egypt, Greece, India, and China—all while in a trance and without physically changing locations. Cayce also claimed he could travel to the future. In early 1929 he predicted the October stock market crash that plunged the country into the Great Depression. In 1935 the Sleeping Prophet predicted World War II would start within four years. The war began in Europe in 1939. Cayce's predictions were not always right, however. In 1934 he predicted that earthquakes and tidal waves would bring a catastrophic end to life on earth in the year 1998.

Cayce made 14,000 predictions before his death in 1945. The prophecies are now stored in a library at the foundation he started, the Association for Research and Enlightenment in Virginia.

Smith's Martian Cycles attracted the attention of a Swiss psychologist named Théodore Flournoy, who was studying clairvoyant phenomena. Flournoy learned to assist Smith during her space travels, helping her as she fell into a trance state and writing down her communications. Flournoy described the Martian Cycles in the 1891 book *From India to the Planet Mars*.

Although Flournoy had assisted Smith for several years, he was highly critical of her in his book. Flournoy was not convinced that the Martian medium was genuine. He described her words and writing as products of subconscious fantasies and a deep need to satisfy the desires of her followers. In simpler terms, Flournoy believed Smith was playing to her audience and providing them with a good show. After the book was published, Smith refused to let Flournoy witness her séances.

By the end of the 1890s Smith began what was called a Hindu Cycle in which she wrote and communicated in Sanskrit, a language unknown to her. Smith also developed her talents as a painter, creating landscapes of Mars. These were created using what might be called automatic painting, in which Smith simply painted on a canvas without planning or thinking.

Smith's Surrealism

In the early 1900s French writer and poet André Breton became a fan of Smith's spirit communications and automatic paintings. This inspired Breton to launch a new literary and art movement called surrealism. Like Smith's work, surrealism was based on setting dreamlike, otherworldly images against starkly realistic ones. Breton described surrealism as the "fusion of elements of fantasy with elements of the modern world to form a kind of superior reality."[15] Smith's description of Mars as a place with aircraft and dogs that can write blends fantasy and elements of reality.

Because of her inspiration to the movement, surrealists referred to Smith as the "Muse of Automatic Writing." In 1928 Breton wrote a surrealist novel called *Nadja*. The book, composed by automatic writing, uses the term "Hélène Smith" not as a name but as a phrase that means amazing. Anything that was the result of a marvelous visionary inspiration, be it a painting, play, or song was a "Hélène Smith."

Smith died in 1929. While it remains unknown whether her Martian Cycles were subconscious fantasies or clairvoyance, Smith's name is now associated with surrealism, an artistic movement that influenced generations of artists.

Clairaudient Transmissions

Smith often experienced clairaudience, for "clear hearing." While Smith heard the Martian language or Sanskrit in her "inner ear," other clairaudients perceive music and other sounds. Instances of clairaudience have been documented throughout history by shamans, prophets, and others who have claimed to hear cosmic voices. For example, in the Bible, Jesus delivers the first prophecies of Revelation to John in a loud trumpet-like blast.

Psychics believe clairaudience consists of sounds that are cosmic vibrations produced by the soul. Sometimes the sounds are physical, that is, plainspoken voices of spirits that are easily understood. These sounds have been described as audible thoughts, mind speech, or astral voices. Physical sounds are not necessarily human voices. They might be bells, flutes, organs, animal noises, the roar of the ocean, running water, or other sounds of nature. Nonphysical clairaudience consists of unclear or obscure noises, humming, static, or buzzing.

Some clairaudients create poems, plays, and even long novels through automatic writing allegedly dictated by spirits.

Sometimes the writer is in a trance and only vaguely aware of what has been written. Other times the clairaudient is conscious of what is happening.

Hours of Profound Writing

Aura May Hollen was a clairaudient who was wide awake and completely aware when spirits were speaking to her. Hollen's clairaudience began in the summer of 1928 when she was sitting outdoors at a bustling restaurant while on vacation in France. The young woman, who had never written more than letters to friends and family, picked up a pencil and dashed off four poems while waiting for her coffee to cool. She wrote these poems without pausing to consider a particular word or phrase and without making changes in any of the 32 lines in each poem. According to the poet's husband, physician Henry Hollen, in the six weeks that followed, Aura May wrote a total of 170 poems. They were composed on train rides, in hotels and dining rooms, and on ships and boats.

Hollen's poems were published in the book *Flowers of Thought*. Reporter Bailey Millard reviewed the book in the *Los Angeles Times* in 1931 and wrote that Hollen "has been singing in the manner of a disciplined versifier. Words, titles and all, come to her as if out of space. And thus she writes habitually without effort or premeditation."[16]

In 1929 Hollen returned to her home in Los Angeles and wrote several more books of sonnets. Some of them, such as "The Coast of Brittany," describe places she had never visited. At the end of the year Hollen began writing children's stories. During a two-month period she wrote 59 stories—16 of them in a single day. Like the famed

Aesop's Fables, the stories feature animals and end with moral sayings. According to Henry Hollen, the tales were written with little effort:

> Aura May Hollen gives no thought whatsoever to the subject-matter of her writings; nor, in the case of her poems, to the rhyme or to the rhythm. All is prepared extra-cranially [outside the skull] and comes to her mind and consciousness fully elaborated, word for word and line for line. She simply sits down to write when the impulse to do so makes itself felt. . . . The tedium of effort on the mental side, in other words, is absent. There is no weariness even after hours of profound writing.[17]

Listening for the Voice

In 1930, after composing hundreds of poems, Hollen began writing long books about philosophy, spiritualism, Christianity, and paranormal phenomena. During a six-month period, she wrote 10 books containing a total of more than 250,000 words. Henry Hollen describes how the book *Leaves from the Tree of Life* was composed: "The contents of this volume was written in five hours, the first portion while [Aura May] was driving her car from Hollywood to downtown Los Angeles. I transcribed the material as she recited it, in the thick of traffic."[18]

Another book in the series, *Enlightenment*, was written at a rate of 8,000 words a day. While writing the books, Hollen used words, names, dates, and historical details wholly unfamiliar to her. According to her husband, the facts were later verified with dictionaries and encyclopedias. Hollen also wrote of mythical worlds and planets, visions of the universe at its creation, and obscure subjects beyond the realm of the five senses.

Other than receiving page after page of words through clairaudience, Hollen was described as totally normal. According to her husband, she played bridge, went to movies and concerts, and maintained a healthy diet. She never studied writing or poetry in school and, despite writing about spiritual subjects, she was not particularly religious. Hollen did, however, believe that life was continuous and that an individual's soul and spirit lived forever. She believed the soul remembered its ancient roots even as it traveled through time, evolved, and grew. Hollen was convinced she had access to knowledge her soul had gathered over the eons. This gave her what she called "supernormal perception" and provided her with a basis to write an endless stream of poems, stories, and books. The process was described by Henry Hollen: "She feels the call. She answers. She listens for the voice. It is indeed as someone nearby or not so near were speaking, reading aloud, or giving dictation from a finished script; or as if from notes; or wholly improvising on the spot the subject-matter given to be recorded."[19]

Hollen's gift lasted for several years and then stopped as quickly as it had started. Her last published book, with the full title *Golden Precepts from the Book of Life, Embodying the Wisdom of the Eternal Ages, Transcribed by Aura May Hollen*, appeared in 1934. Several of Hollen's books remain in print, and many used editions are available online. Whatever happened to Hollen herself after her six-year burst of prolific clairaudience remains a mystery.

"I Am Already Dead"

Hollen seemed to have a rare gift. She made little effort to encourage her clairaudience, and it did not seem to come from a specific spirit or source. In most cases of clairaudience, mediums deliberately call up individual spirits and ask detailed questions. This was the situation in 2003 when a medium claimed to call up the spirit of a murdered woman in order to hear details of her death.

The story began when Laci Peterson of Modesto, California, went missing around Christmas Day in 2002. Peterson was 27 years old and seven months pregnant, and her disappearance riveted the nation. Hundreds of newspaper articles were written about the missing young mother-to-be, and cable news shows provided full coverage of every twist and turn in the case.

In California, police, friends, family, and concerned neighbors initiated a massive search for Peterson. A reward of up to $500,000 was offered for any information leading to her safe return. Friends launched a website which attracted over 1,000 volunteers. Bulletin boards and utility poles across the state were plastered with fliers asking for help in the case.

Police suspected foul play, and by mid-January authorities were focused on the actions of Laci's husband, Scott Peterson. Scott claimed that on the day his wife disappeared he was fishing for sturgeon 90 miles (144km) from Modesto on San Francisco Bay, near the Berkeley Marina. Police had doubts about parts of his story.

In North Carolina, a psychic detective named Noreen Renier followed the Laci Peterson case as it unfolded. Psychic detectives say they use the powers of clairvoyance to help solve crimes, and Renier claimed she had participated in over 600 cases worldwide. In early January 2003, Renier says, she received dozens of e-mails from people who wanted her help locating Laci Peterson. Renier declined, later writing, "it was a police case and I would have to be invited to work on the case by either the family or the police."[20]

Several weeks later, Renier was contacted by a family member. Scott's mother, Jackie Peterson, hired the psychic detective in an effort to prove her son's innocence in his wife's disappearance.

By early March 2003 Laci Peterson was still missing, but police did not have enough evidence to classify the case as a murder investigation. On March 2 Renier went into a psychic trance and began channeling Laci. In the taped transcript of the session the spirit of Laci purportedly spoke through Renier, declaring, "I am already dead."[21] Although she did not name her killer, the spirit of

A psychic claimed to have made contact with Laci Peterson about two months after the Modesto woman's mysterious disappearance. During that contact, involving clairvoyant visions, Peterson (whose photo is displayed during a 2003 memorial service) reportedly described how she was killed.

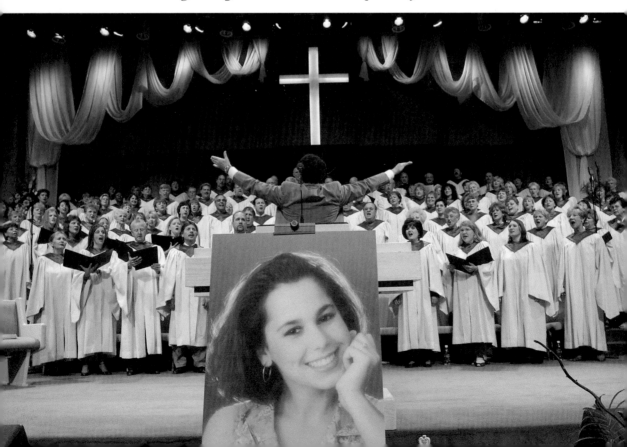

Laci described how her body was disposed of. She said she was in a vehicle covered with a rug or cloth, and it was very early morning. The vehicle moved through intersections, past billboards, and through an older section of town on a state highway numbered 14 or 41. The vehicle made a U-turn and stopped at a large body of fresh water near a park. The spirit said she heard the unidentified killer say: "I'm putting her into the water with cement. It's around her. It's for her to sink."[22] The spirit then told Renier she was lying in sand beneath a rushing body of water where there was a fishy odor.

Many Clues, Vague Statements

Renier wrote down the details of her psychic detective session and mailed them to a Modesto police detective, Charles Grogan. It is unknown whether Grogan read the report or used it in any way. About six weeks later, on April 14, the body of Laci Peterson was discovered in San Francisco Bay. It had washed ashore at Point Isabel Regional Shoreline Park in Richmond, California. This was only 5 miles (8km) from where Scott Peterson claimed to be fishing the day Laci disappeared. Scott was arrested four days later. He was subsequently convicted of killing Laci Peterson and given the death penalty.

Some of Renier's clairvoyant visions seemed to be correct. According to police reports, Laci's body was hidden in the back of Scott's SUV and taken to a park. She was loaded into his fishing boat, which likely had a fishy smell. Police later revealed that a cement anchor had been attached to Laci's body. However, some parts of Renier's session were incorrect. Laci was not found in freshwater but in the salty San Francisco Bay. There was no highway 14 or 41 nearby. However, Laci was found on April 14.

Skeptics point out that Scott Peterson was a suspect from the

start, and it was public knowledge that he was fishing in Berkeley around the time of Laci's disappearance. It would not have taken a clairvoyant to guess what might have happened to Laci. As Joe Nickell, of *Skeptical Inquirer* magazine points out, clairvoyants throw out many clues and once a case is solved match up the vague statements to the facts. As Nickell writes, "No psychic found Laci Peterson."[23] However, Renier's contributions to the case brought her a degree of fame. She was interviewed by several newspapers and appeared on TV news shows. Renier also wrote a book about the Peterson case and others she had worked on.

Crisis Apparitions

Most instances of spirit communication are not as dramatic as the Laci Peterson case. Many times spirits speak unbidden, and those who claim to hear them are not professional psychics. Since the 1930s the Parapsychology Lab at Duke University has documented over 14,000 cases of unprompted spirit contact. The incidents most often involve a recently deceased person contacting a parent, sibling, other relative, or close friend. These spirits are called crisis apparitions because they appear at the moment of death during times of violence, disasters, and other crises.

Crisis apparitions are most often recorded during wartime. There are hundreds of documented cases of mothers "seeing" and "speaking" to their sons who were killed thousands of miles away on a battlefield. Sally Rhine Feather, daughter of Louisa and Joseph Banks Rhine and director of the Rhine Researcher Center, believes crisis apparitions are a result of shared clairvoyance between family members and close friends. She explains why the apparitions often appear during war:

War generates intense emotions of fear and anxiety for soldiers. "Will I be killed?" "Will I be injured?" "Will I ever make it home again to see the people I love?" Meanwhile, the same emotional worries and fears haunt loved ones back home. Both share a desperate desire to communicate with each other in times of danger, to exchange news, solace, and support. . . . Given this intense emotional need to contact a loved one, we shouldn't be surprised to find ESP sometimes fills that gap when normal communication channels are slow or unavailable.[24]

Not all crisis apparitions are a result of violence. Some occur when a person dies unexpectedly. Donna Stewart, a psi investigator in Coos Bay, Oregon, claims to have experienced a crisis apparition in the early 1980s when she was only 7 years old. As Donna recalls, her best friend Danny lived next door. One day Danny was stricken with a minor illness, tonsillitis, and was taken to the hospital to have his tonsils removed. Donna wished her friend a speedy recovery but thought little else of it.

"Given this intense emotional need to contact a loved one, we shouldn't be surprised to find ESP sometimes fills that gap when normal communication channels are slow or unavailable."
—ESP researcher Sally Rhine Feather.

The next day, Donna was in her bedroom alone when she looked up and saw Danny standing at the foot of her bed. He spoke, asking her if she wanted to play in the yard. Donna left the room to get her mother's permission to go outside with Danny. Stewart says her mother "went white. She told me that wasn't possible. Danny had an allergic reaction during surgery and died. When I went back to my room, he was gone."[25]

Donna's ESP experience included clairaudience, as she was able to hear Danny speak. Believers say that crisis apparitions often offer comforting words to the living, say good-bye, or explain the details of their deaths.

Psychic Smelling and Tasting

Some who experience clairaudience also report smelling pleasant odors such as perfume or flowers. This most often occurs during séances moments before a medium channels a spirit voice. When an aroma is part of a clairvoyant experience it is called clairalience, or "clear smelling." Reported examples of the phenomenon include smelling the perfume of a deceased aunt or the cigar smoke of a dead uncle. According to psychic Astoria Brown, "It's very common for the room to fill with the scent of a beloved family member or friend when partaking in a séance. . . . [This] is validation that the deceased loved one is certainly present and is making their visitation clearly known to all that are attending the meeting."[26]

In some cases psychic smells are accompanied by flavors, an experience known as clairgustance, or "clear tasting." This form of ESP allows psychics to experience a wide variety of taste sensations from beyond the physical realm. During séances people have made claims that they tasted cupcakes like those made by their deceased grandmothers. Others recalled tasting the tea a dead aunt used to serve. Whether this is wishful thinking or spirits communicating from beyond the grave remains a matter of debate.

Psychic detectives might try to draw on the power of clairgus-

"QUOTE"

"It's very common for the room to fill with the scent of a beloved family member or friend when partaking in a séance."

—Psychic Astoria Brown.

tance when working to solve crimes. In such cases, the psychic might taste blood, drugs, alcohol, or poisonous chemicals while in a trance. These sensations provide clues to crimes in which victims might have been beaten, drugged, or poisoned.

Fantasy-Prone People

Skeptics say that people who taste, smell, hear, see, or feel spirits have what is known as a fantasy-prone personality (FPP). This condition, described by psychologists Sheryl C. Wilson and Theodore X. Barber in 1981, is applied to otherwise normal people who believe they have mystical powers. People with FPP might believe they are solving crimes or even visiting Mars.

Those who believe in clairvoyance dismiss the FPP concept. They point to thousands of unexplained clairvoyant experiences that have been verified over the years by researchers. As Feather writes, clairvoyance "continues to manifest itself spontaneously in peoples' lives, in consistent, familiar ways that suggest a universal, human phenomenon."[27] While the controversy over clairvoyance continues, one point is not in doubt. The human mind, emotions, and senses are extremely powerful and operate in many ways not yet understood by science.

CHAPTER 3

Extrasensory Warfare

In 1960 a headline in the French magazine *Science and Life (Science et Vie)* screamed in all capital letters: US NAVY USES ESP ON AN ATOMIC SUB! The article asserted that sailors on the world's first nuclear-powered submarine, *Nautilus*, had conducted successful experiments in mental telepathy. The article posed three alarming questions: "Is telepathy the new secret weapon? Will ESP be a deciding factor in future warfare? Has the American military learned the secret of mind power?"[28]

While the tone of the article might seem comical to modern ears, the magazine appeared on newsstands during the Cold War. At the time, the United States and the Soviet Union (present-day Russia) were amassing a growing arsenal of deadly nuclear missiles. A nuclear war between the superpowers threatened the entire world.

The idea that ESP and the secret of mind power could become part of the nuclear arms race frightened many of those who heard about it. The article did not escape the notice of intelligence officials in the Soviet Union. After reading it, a leading Soviet scientist, L.L. Vasilev, told a group of top Soviet researchers that ESP research must accelerate: "Today the American Navy is testing telepathy on their atomic submarines. Soviet scientists conducted a great many successful telepathy tests over a quarter of a century ago. . . . We must again plunge into the exploration of this vital field."[29]

Vasilev was referring to ESP experiments conducted by the Soviet Union in the 1930s. In one grim test, several baby rabbits were taken aboard a submarine while the mother rabbit was hundreds of miles away in a lab with electrodes attached to her head. Soviet researcher Pavel Naumov describes the research: "When the sub was deep below the surface of the ocean, assistants killed the young rabbits one by one. The mother rabbit obviously didn't know what was happening. . . . Yet, at each synchronized instant of death, her brain reacted. There was communication."[30]

The Psychic Arms Race

American intelligence agents learned about the Soviet ESP experiments after World War II. As the Cold War accelerated throughout the 1950s, a psychic arms race also developed. Both sides sought to gain advantage over the other in the nonphysical world. The psychic arms race led superpower intelligence agencies to study ESP methods that included telepathy and remote viewing. Experiments were conducted not to guess cards but to control minds and mentally spy on top secret military bases.

Some in the American military worried that the Soviets were building nuclear bombs faster than their American counterparts.

At the height of the Cold War, a French magazine claimed that experiments in mental telepathy were being conducted on the USS Nautilus (pictured). Reports of ESP experiments being done by the Soviet Union also circulated during the Cold War.

Others suggested they were training a greater number of tele-paths. These fears were described in the 1970 best-selling book *Psychic Discoveries Behind the Iron Curtain*, which stated that the Soviets had built an army of 2 million psychics trained to conquer the world. In the US Congress, some representatives de-manded that the CIA and other intelligence services close what they called the "psycho-gap" between the superpowers. This meant training more psychics so the United States did not fall behind its mortal enemy.

While working to close the psycho-gap, the CIA conducted a number of tests on unwitting volunteers. Many of the experiments were later deemed immoral and illegal. For example, in 1953, test subjects in a CIA program called Project MK-ULTRA were given massive doses of LSD and other psychedelic drugs. During periods of hallucinations they were subjected to torturous mental programming techniques meant to break down the will. This was intended to produce brainwashed assassins who could be ordered to kill from afar. As part of the program researchers also explored ways that such drugs could be used to increase the powers of mental telepathy. Such powers would be used for remote mind control to regulate the behavior of enemies and programmed assassins.

Artificial Telepathy

MK-ULTRA was never successful, and the project was strongly condemned when its existence was made public by Congress in 1975. The program, with its reliance on drugs, was only one aspect of the military's desire to develop a new kind of telepathy. Others focused on the use of electronic technology meant to create or enhance ESP in test subjects. This concept was referred to by the Pentagon as artificial telepathy.

Artificial telepathy experiments involved beaming radio waves, such as microwaves and UHF and VHF waves, at test subjects. The experiments were conducted in the hope that the invisible waves could send signals to the mind as if it were a mental radio. When artificial telepathy experiments were conducted in the early 1960s, UHF and VHF waves were used to broadcast television signals. Low-level microwaves are widely used today

Walking Through Walls

Albert Stubblebine was a major general in the US Army between 1981 and 1984. He believed soldiers could be trained to walk through walls. Author Jon Ronson describes a failed Stubblebine attempt to apport through a solid wall:

> Major General Albert Stubblebine III is sitting behind his desk in Arlington, Virginia, and he is staring at his wall. . . . There is something he feels he needs to do even though the thought of it frightens him. He thinks about the choice he has to make. He can stay in his office or he can go into the next office. . . .
>
> He stands up, moves out from behind his desk and begins to walk.
>
> *I mean*, he thinks to himself, *what is the*

in digital wireless systems such as cell phones. In 1962 these radio waves were the basis of an artificial telepathy program called MK-DELTA, or Project Deep Sleep. The waves were broadcast to volunteers who were miles away in the hope that the beams would silently transmit spoken words to a subject's brain. In early *atom mostly made up of anyway? Space!*

He quickens his pace.

What am I mostly made up of? he thinks. *Atoms!*

He is almost at a jog now.

What is the wall mostly made up of? he thinks.

Atoms! All I have to do is merge the spaces. The wall is an illusion. What is destiny? Am I destined to stay in this room? Ha, no!

Then General Stubblebine bangs his nose hard on the wall of his office.

Jon Ronson, *The Men Who Stare at Goats*. New York: Simon & Schuster, 2004, pp. 2–3.

tests microwave hearing (as it was known) succeeded in transmitting knocking and buzzing sounds.

Research into microwave hearing was conducted by the Defense Advanced Projects Research Agency (DARPA) between 1965 and the early 1970s. The agency set up Operation PANDORA to continue research into artificial telepathy. According to declassified papers released in 1995 by the US government, Richard Cesaro, director of DARPA, confirmed the initial goal of PANDORA was to "discover whether a carefully controlled microwave signal could control the mind."[31]

While researchers were never able to control minds with microwaves, they did have some success with telepathic microwave communications. In 1973 scientist Joseph C. Sharp was isolated in a soundproof room at Walter Reed Hospital in Washington, DC. Single-syllable spoken words were broadcast through heavy bursts of microwaves. Sharp was able to identify the words in his mind without any form of electronic translation device. This type of direct transmission of microwaves to the brain is called voice-to-skull communication. However, the experiments were discontinued because the voice-to-skull experiments used high-energy microwaves that could have endangered Sharp's life if used for prolonged periods.

"Raise No Questions"

While some branches of the government worked to develop technology for artificial telepathy, the CIA attempted to perfect the traditional form of ESP known as remote viewing. Like the artificial telepathy programs, RV research was cloaked in secrecy, but for different reasons. Mind-reading microwave machines were considered top secret weapons that could be used to kill. Remote-viewing research was classified as secret because it might have caused the government great embarrassment. CIA officials worried that skeptics in Congress and the general public would mock the agency and call for the program to be shut down if its cost became known. At the time, the CIA was spending millions of dollars a year on its experiments with remote viewing ESP.

The top secret nature of the RV experiments was revealed in a CIA memo made public in 1978. The unnamed author of the memo, which dated back to the 1950s, stated: "[The CIA will] push psi research as far and as fast as we can reasonably do in the direction of practical application . . . while being exceedingly careful about thorough cloaking of the under-taking. Funds necessary for the support of the work would . . . carry no identification and raise no questions."[32] To keep the pro-gram secret—even from the psychics who were test subjects—the agency conducted experiments through universities and small re-search institutes. In order to cloak their intentions the CIA rarely used the term ESP, preferring the tongue-twisting phrase "novel biological information transfer" instead.

Testing the Accuracy of Psychics

Remote viewing became the central focus of a CIA study begun in May 1973. Two scientists, Harold Puthoff and Russell Targ, de-signed Project Scanate to pit psychics against secret agents. The program, established at the Stanford Research Institute (SRI) in California, was calculated to test whether remote viewers were more accurate than spies or top secret satellite photos.

During Project Scanate, personnel at the CIA selected targets all over the world, including classified military sites in the Soviet Union, China, and even the United States. General map coordi-nates for the unnamed sites were sent anonymously to research-ers monitoring the Scanate project at SRI. This process ensured that no one outside the CIA knew the exact details of the selected targets. In some cases, selected sites in the Soviet Union were those that had not yet been photographed by spy satellites. After remote viewers envisioned the sites, the sites were photographed and compared with the initial reports from the psychics.

Puthoff and Targ believed that with training, almost anyone could develop powers of ESP and become what they called a psychic spy. Rather than recruit professional clairvoyants, they chose to work with people who were living near the SRI. Early program volunteers included a freelance photographer, two SRI staff members, and a scientist working at the facility. One recruit, Richard Bach, was a renowned author who had written the best seller *Jonathan Livingston Seagull*.

Spy or Psychic?

One of the psychic spies in Project Scanate recruited himself. Pat Price read a magazine article about ESP experiments being conducted at the SRI (but not the CIA connection). Price was a former police commissioner of Burbank, California, who claimed to have strong psychic gifts that he had used in the past to catch criminals. Puthoff was skeptical about Price's assertions but gave him map coordinates over the phone for a secret government facility located in Virginia.

Several days after accepting the challenge, Price delivered a five-page report with details of his psychic spying. Price claimed he first viewed facilities from 1,500 feet (457m) in the air before swooping down to enter the building and explore its interior. Price's report listed specific types of office equipment and names displayed on desk nameplates. The report identified the facility as one run by the Army Signal Corps. This shadowy branch of the military manages intelligence and command and control commu-

A Soviet missile, normally hidden in secret facilities, rolls down a street during a 1960s military parade. During a remote-viewing session, psychic spy Pat Price mapped buildings and tunnels of what turned out to be a previously unknown Soviet missile construction facility.

nications, much of it top secret. To Puthoff's amazement, Price also included the names he read on labels of file folders locked in filing cabinets including "Cue Ball," "Four Ball," "Eight Ball," "Rackup," and "Side Pocket."

The details provided by Price seemed more like the products of a good imagination than of ESP, but Puthoff sent Price's report to the CIA anyway. Several weeks later the agency informed Puthoff that the file names provided by Price were indeed related to various secret Signal Corps projects. As Ken Kress, the CIA agent working with the Scanate Project, wrote in an official memorandum: "Price, who had no military or intelligence background, provided a list of project titles associated with current and past activities including one of extreme sensitivity. Also, the codename of the site was provided. Other information concerning the physical layout of the site was accurate."[33]

The astonishing revelations marked Price as a possible Soviet spy, prompting the CIA to launch an intensive investigation into his life and activities. As it turned out, Price was not a spy, but some questioned his sanity. During interrogations, Price said he could use his mind to evaporate rain clouds and make red traffic lights turn green. In addition, Price claimed he could psychically see UFOs, and he readily identified secret alien space bases he said were located in many countries across the globe.

Despite his outlandish claims, Price made himself useful to Project Scanate. In one experiment, Price created startlingly accurate, detailed sketches of a Soviet military base. During a remote-viewing session, Price saw massive cranes and mobile gantries (frameworks that hold machinery). One gantry was on railroad tracks that went into an underground building. Price said the machinery was on a Soviet military base 25 to 30 miles (40km to 48km) south of the Irtysh River in Siberia. During his remote-viewing sessions, Price drew a map that contained the layout of buildings and tunnels at the facility. Satellite photos taken by the CIA later proved that Price was once again right and that the previously unknown facility was being used for missile construction.

Instant Death

CIA Director Stansfield Turner never took his agency's psi programs seriously, believing they were a waste of resources. This was not the case in the Soviet Union. According to intelligence reports, the Soviets tirelessly experimented with the training of psychic spies, and their efforts went far beyond simple remote viewing.

The Soviets tried to develop an ESP-related technique for moving physical objects through space. The apport technique, as it became known, was based on the concept of out-of-body experiences (OBE), or astral travel. The astral body is said to be an energy force that every person possesses, and it can temporarily leave the physical body behind and travel throughout the universe. When doing so the astral body appears to the human eye as a luminous cloud. Sorcerers and psychics have long claimed the power to project their astral bodies into adjoining rooms, through walls, to other continents, or even other planets.

The Soviet theory behind the apport technique takes the concept of an astral body one step further. According to this theory, astral bodies can do more than travel through space; they can also move physical objects through space. In addition, the astral body can cause physical harm. A declassified US Defense Intelligence Agency (DIA) report from 1995 imagines a Soviet agent utilizing the apport technique:

> [The] psychic subject transports his "energy body" to a remote site, dematerializes an object, then transports it back and materializes it. . . . There has been some discussion recently about the prospects of being able to control the apport technique to a point of sophistication where individuals could . . . produce instant death in military and civilian officials.

It is further conjectured that these bodies could disable military equipment or communications.[34]

In 1976 Nikolai Khokhlov, a former Soviet intelligence agent, defected to the United States. He told the CIA that the Soviets had spent hundreds of millions of dollars to establish 20 top secret underground research laboratories to study apport techniques and various ESP phenomena. The labs employed hundreds of the nation's leading scientists. Khokhlov claimed that Soviet psi research involved brutal experiments conducted on prisoners. Victims were subjected to hypnosis, sleep deprivation, drugs, and electrical charges that often disrupted brain waves or paralyzed nerves.

Fighting Enemy Submarines

Some in the US intelligence community believed Khokhlov was a double agent who continued to work for the Soviets. It was thought that his grand descriptions of Soviet ESP research were what agents referred to as disinformation. If so, Khokhlov was providing false information to trick the United States into spending millions of dollars on ESP studies. Beyond the monetary costs, the Soviets might have also been trying to convince the military to use America's leading scientists to research nonexistent phenomena.

Whether or not Khokhlov was providing disinformation, the United States continued studying ESP. However, the efforts were largely confined to low-key, inexpensive research. For example, in 1977 the navy paid the SRI around $50,000 to determine whether psychics could detect flashing lights or electrical pulses at a distance. If this were possible, then psychics might be able to detect the location of enemy submarines.

Another low-cost study was conducted to see whether psychics could use their mental powers to stop a magnetometer. Magnetometers, which measure the strength of a magnetic field, are placed on the ocean floor in various locations to monitor submarine activity. When a submarine passes nearby, the metal on the vessel triggers a response on the magnetometer. Apparently some of the psychics at the SRI were able to disrupt magnetometers. This prompted Joel Larson, a navy scientist involved with the experiment, to state: "I have always believed that ESP is the only way to fight submarines. The magnetometer tests were designed to prove that principle."[35]

The Stargate Project

The navy studies were part of a government ESP research program called the Stargate Project. This top secret program was backed by the CIA and the DIA. It lasted two decades, from 1975 to 1995, and encompassed many RV research projects with unusual names, such as Operations Grill Flame, Center Lane, Gondola Wish, and Sun Streak.

One of the most critical tests for the Stargate remote viewers came in late 1979 after 52 Americans working at the US embassy in Tehran, Iran, were taken hostage by Islamist students and militants. The hostage crisis riveted the attention of the world as armed Iranian students paraded the blindfolded and handcuffed Americans through the streets. The hostage crisis lasted 444 days and included an embarrassing failed rescue attempt by the US military.

Some months after the crisis began, a remote viewer known only as Viewer Number 66 went to work for Operation Grill Flame. The mission was to envision the American hostages and their Iranian captors. During an RV exercise, Viewer Number 66 mentally floated above a building and through a door with Arabic

> **"QUOTE"**
>
> "I have always believed that ESP is the only way to fight submarines."
>
> —Navy scientist Joel Larson.

writing on it. The viewer observed a large gathering of people, young students led by an older man. Viewer Number 66 determined that the meeting was about the American hostages. The RV monitor asked if the Iranians intended to kill the hostages. Viewer Number 66 answered:

> No! No, they are not talking about that. The conversation seems to be centering on what to do with them . . . let me see . . . to keep them here or to put them somewhere else. In fact, the old man is upset about the way some of them [the hostages] have been treated. He thinks the young people have abused them, and he is cautioning them to take better care of the hostages. I'm getting tired now . . . I think I want to come back now. Is that okay? I want to come back.[36]

As it turned out, the hostages were not treated well by the student militants. While older leaders might or might not have called for better treatment, the hostages were kept chained and bound for weeks at a time. They were beaten, repeatedly threatened, and subjected to mock executions. However, all of the hostages survived the ordeal and were released in January 1981.

"Am I in Space?"

In 1988 Viewer Number 66's top secret report about the hostage crisis was shown to David Morehouse, a former Army Ranger. Like Viewer Number 66, Morehouse often had visions of floating above city streets, passing through doors and walls, and even traveling in time. However, unlike trained remote viewers, Morehouse's experiences began spontaneously after he was wounded by a stray machine gun bullet while on a training mission. More-house thought he was losing his mind when he began to have haunting nightmares and unexplainable visions of events in the past, present, and future. When he described his visions to his superiors, he was recruited by the DIA and put to work as a re-mote viewer on the classified program Sun Streak conducted at Fort Meade in Maryland.

As part of the Sun Streak program, remote viewers like More-house were closely monitored. Instruments checked their body

The US military tested psychic ability to disable a magnetometer, a device that can monitor submarine activity when placed on the ocean floor. The study apparently revealed that some psychics could disrupt the devices, which are also used (as shown) in undersea archaeological and other expeditions.

functions, including respiration, pulse, temperature, and brain-waves. This was done to prevent panic attacks after one remote viewer nearly suffered a heart attack from her experience.

Video cameras and microphones recorded every move and word from Morehouse. Headphones played classical music such as Beethoven's *Moonlight* Sonata to promote a hypnotic state. According to Morehouse, as the sessions began he reclined in a chair, relaxed, and "jumped into the ether."[37] Despite the calming conditions, Morehouse was often frightened during remote viewing sessions, as he makes clear in one description:

Time had nearly stopped. I felt myself rising into darkness, away from the table and the room. Up, up . . . I tried to gain some sense of what and where I was. There was a rushing sound in my ears, like a cold wind passing. I felt blind, helpless, and cold. Pinholes of light came into focus, like stars in a black fog. *Am I in space?*. . . The "stars" suddenly blurred into horizontal streaks of light. I felt myself accelerating faster and faster, falling toward the target as if through a tunnel of light. My speed began to create heat around me, and I closed my eyes and fists, expecting them to burn.[38]

After tense moments Morehouse finally relaxed and allowed himself to be guided by his monitors in sessions that could last two to three hours. However, the grueling sessions had negative effects on Morehouse's mental health. During one test, he was taken to a World War II Nazi concentration camp. The sight and smell of the hundreds of dead bodies he envisioned gave him nightmares for months.

In 1991, after Iraq invaded Kuwait, the United States intervened to eject the Iraqi troops. Morehouse claims that during the war his monitors took him to a battlefield in Kuwait. As he flew through the air, all he could see was burning oil wells. He even choked on the smoke he envisioned. Within weeks, Morehouse's remote vision seemingly had come true. As the Iraqis were driven out of Kuwait by American forces, they set fire to more than 700 oil wells, which took months to extinguish.

Staring at Goats

Not long after Morehouse traveled to Kuwait in the ether, the Soviet Union collapsed, bringing an end to the Cold War psychic arms race. Project Stargate continued until 1995 when an analysis of the program was conducted by a team of respected scientists at the American Institute for Research (AIR). A report written by AIR concluded that correct hits by remote viewers were higher than chance would warrant. However, it was not clear whether this was due to correct guessing or paranormal abilities in the viewers. The AIR report concluded that Project Stargate should be discontinued.

After the military discontinued Stargate, it was no longer classified as top secret. A number of books and articles were published that described America's psychic warfare programs. After a few years, psychic warfare was largely forgotten by the general public. However, the programs were in the news again in 2004 after filmmaker and author Jon Ronson wrote *The Men Who Stare at Goats*. According to the book, in 1979 an army lieutenant colonel named Jim Channon tried to convince the military to form a super fighting force called the First Earth Battalion. The hypothetical military unit would be staffed by specially trained officers who used their mental powers to perform paranormal tasks

as described by Ronson: "[Soldiers would] attain the power to pass through objects such as walls, bend metal with their minds, walk on fire, calculate faster than a computer, stop their own hearts with no ill effects, see into the future, have out-of-body experiences . . . and be able to hear and see other people's thoughts."[39]

Those in the First Earth Battalion would also be able to kill without touching an enemy. In order to train for this exercise, the military established a top secret Goat Lab at Fort Bragg in North Carolina. Some of the soldiers who trained there allegedly were able to stare at goats until the animals dropped dead from heart attacks.

Knowing All, Seeing All

The Men Who Stare at Goats was turned into a film starring George Clooney in 2009. If the US military were training psychic warriors at that time it remained a closely guarded secret. However, many of the remote viewers who once worked for the government have remained active. Some offer remote viewing courses that cost several thousand dollars. Organizations such as the International Remote Viewing Association have websites and publish newsletters, magazines, blogs, and books. While remote viewers are no longer employed by the CIA, hundreds of people continue to claim the ability to travel through time at will.

CHAPTER 4

Dreaming of the Future

In May 1902 a London-based aeronautical engineer named John William Dunne had a disturbingly vivid dream. He seemed to be standing on a sloping hill, high on a mountain. Small fissures beneath his feet spewed jets of foul-smelling steam. He realized he was on an island, standing on a volcano. Dunne described his thoughts: "Good Lord, the whole thing is going to *blow up!*"[40] In his dream, Dunne felt a sudden frantic desire to save the island's 4,000 inhabitants from an impending volcanic explosion. (He knew the exact number of inhabitants.) As often happens in dreams, the scene suddenly shifted. Dunne now perceived himself to be on a neighboring island where he was trying to convince French officials to send a fleet of rescue boats to the endangered island. He claims he awoke screaming, "Listen! Four thousand people will be killed!"[41]

The next morning the headlines in the London *Daily Telegraph* read "Volcano Disaster in Martinique, Town Swept Away . . . Probable Loss of over 40,000 Lives."[42] The article explained that Martinique's Mount Pelée, which had been dormant for more than a century, had unexpectedly erupted, killing thousands.

Dunne was intrigued by his dream but puzzled that the death toll was off by a factor of ten. This led him to conclude that when he dreamed of the Mount Pelée eruption he had already read the newspaper article about the disaster—but in the future. In addition, he had misread the headline and mistakenly thought it said 4,000 deaths occurred rather than 40,000.

After his disaster dream, Dunne developed a theory that the past, present, and future exist all at once. However, the human mind can only comprehend this while dreaming. According to this theory, dreams are inspired by both future and past events. According to Dunne, "Dreams in general, all dreams, everybody's dreams [are] composed of images of past experiences and images of future experiences blended together in approximately equal proportions."[43]

Dunne's theories about the past and the future led him to a lifelong study of his dreams. After writing down dozens of dreams upon awakening, he discovered that about one in ten, or 10 percent, represented future events. Some of the dreams were about trivial occurrences, others about events that were important enough to appear in newspapers. In 1927 Dunne described his dreams in the influential book *An Experiment with Time*.

A hand-colored photograph shows the devastating 1902 eruption of Mount Pelée on the Caribbean island of Martinique. A London aeronautical engineer claimed to have dreamed about the event the night before it occurred in what has since come to be known as a precognitive dream.

Precognitive Dreams

Dunne's work was based on a type of ESP known as precognitive dreams. Precognition, or knowing something before it happens, is also referred to as future sight. Those who experience precognition have vivid visions of events which have not yet taken place. While precognition may occur while awake, researchers at the Rhine Institute found that it mostly happens in dreams. Of the 3,290 precognitive experiences studied at the institute, 68 percent happened during sleep.

Precognitive dreams are quite common. A 2011 study by *Psychology Today* noted that about 50 percent of the general public reported recently experiencing at least one precognitive dream. These dreams may be broken down into three categories: prophetic, warning, and telepathic. Prophetic dreams are those in which future events are simply revealed or foretold. Warning dreams foretell a future calamity while presenting ways for the dreamer to prevent or alter the outcome. Telepathic dreams are like crisis apparitions, but they occur when the receiver is asleep: A person who is sick, dying, or recently dead appears in a dream to deliver a message.

Unlike card guessing or remote viewing, precognitive dreams are nearly impossible to study in a scientific manner. Oftentimes those who claim to have had dreams about actual shipwrecks, mining accidents, terrorist attacks, or other great catastrophes only come forward after the disaster has occurred. In addition, precognitive dreams can occur many days before an actual event, so they are often dismissed by the dreamers. As scientist and professional skeptic Martin Gardner explains:

> Most dreams contain a wealth of vaguely defined, unrelated events. It is impossible to know how many events in a precognitive dream were quickly forgotten because they had no relation to any waking events in the near future. . . . [There is also a] time-lag between a precognitive dream and the event. Many such dreams occur several days, sometimes even weeks, before the dramatic event. This means we have to consider all the events that occurred in all of the person's dreams over what may be a substantial number of days.[44]

Skeptics reject the validity of precognitive dreams, saying that dreams that predict the future are simply coincidental. They point out that an average person has about a dozen dreams a night, most of which are instantly forgotten. That means that on any given night, countless people are likely to be dreaming about catastrophes. Greek philosopher Aristotle addressed this in the fourth century BC, saying, "[People] have many visions of all kinds; they can be expected to strike lucky now and again."[45]

"Who Is Dead in the White House?"

Many of the visions that occur in dreams are based on common fears such as falling, drowning, and being chased. Some people even dream about their own deaths. In one famous case, the dreamer was the president of the United States, and his death was one of the most famous events in American history.

Abraham Lincoln presided over a nation divided by the Civil War, which began in 1861 not long after he was sworn in as president. In the ensuing four years, more than 620,000 Americans were killed. Although the war was winding down in early 1865, Lincoln was still occupied by his role as commander in chief of the Union Army. One night in early April, while waiting for important dispatches from the front, Lincoln fell into a fitful sleep. He soon began to dream that he heard weeping. In the dream, Lincoln left his bed and followed the sounds of pitiful sobbing until he came to the East Room of the White House. The president saw a coffin holding a corpse. Lincoln explains the rest of his precognitive dream:

> Around it were stationed soldiers who were act-
> ing as guards; and there was a throng of people,

some gazing mournfully upon the corpse, whose face was covered, others weeping pitifully. "Who is dead in the White House?" I demanded of one of the soldiers. "The President," was his answer; "he was killed by an assassin!" Then came a loud burst of grief from the crowd, which awoke me from my dream. I slept no more that night; and although it was only a dream, I have been strangely annoyed by it ever since.[46]

Lincoln told his close friend Ward Hill Lamon about the dream. Several weeks later, the scene from Lincoln's dream became reality. On April 14, 1865, the president was shot in the head and killed by John Wilkes Booth.

Lamon described Lincoln's dream in an 1895 book he wrote about the president. Lamon went on to write that Lincoln himself alluded to the terrible dream with a degree of humor and believed the dream corpse in the White House belonged to someone else. Whatever the case, skeptics point out that it should surprise no one that Lincoln dreamed of assassination. From his first days in office in 1861, the president received numerous death threats. On one occasion a would-be assassin actually took a shot at the president. The bullet passed through his hat, missing his head by inches.

The Dramatic Sinking of the *Titanic*

While Lincoln's assassination might have been anticipated by some, few people believed the luxurious British ocean liner RMS *Titanic* would ever sink. The company that built the *Titanic*, White Star Lines, claimed it was unsinkable due to watertight compartments in its hull. When the ship left England on its maiden voyage on April 10, 1912, most passengers undoubtedly expected to return home safely. However, four days into its journey to New York City the *Titanic* sank after hitting an iceberg in the North Atlantic. About 1,520 people lost their lives, while 700 survived.

After the *Titanic* tragedy, a number of people claimed they had prophetic, telepathic, or warning dreams about the wreck of the luxury ocean liner. Accounts of the dreams were published in books and journals in the decades that followed. The stories were compiled in a 1960 article by psychiatry professor Ian Stevenson, who writes, "A considerable number of apparently extrasensory experiences occurred in connection with the dramatic sinking of the White Star Liner *Titanic* in April 1912. Some of these were apparently precognitive."[47]

Stevenson describes premonitions by 20 people who said they envisioned the *Titanic* disaster. In an example of a warning dream, a man listed only as Mr. Middleton had two dreams in which he saw the ocean liner sink. In one dream, the ship hit an iceberg. These dreams caused Middleton to cancel his passage on the *Titanic*. However, as Gardner points out, "Because fears of ships hitting icebergs in the North Atlantic were prevalent at the time, dreams of this sort must have been extremely common."[48]

A telepathic dream that occurred to Marianne Gracie while the ship was sinking is harder to explain. Gracie was dreaming hundreds of miles away from the catastrophe in New York City when she heard a command that she should get on her knees and pray for those at sea. Gracie awoke and fell on her knees in prayer. Purportedly, at that exact moment, her husband, Major Archibald

"A considerable number of apparently extrasensory experiences occurred in connection with the dramatic sinking of the White Star Liner *Titanic* in April 1912. Some of these were apparently precognitive."

—Psychiatry professor Ian Stevenson.

Gracie, had just jumped from the sinking *Titanic* into the ocean. The major barely lived through the ordeal by clinging to an overturned lifeboat. He later said that while he was struggling to survive in the frigid water, he sent a mental message to his wife to tell her he was dying and that they would meet again in heaven. He later said that his wife's prayers allowed him to survive.

Astonishing Parallels

While skeptics dismiss such stories as not provable, one premonition was printed in black in white. In 1898, 14 years before the

After the dramatic sinking of the Titanic (depicted in this illustration), accounts surfaced of people who had experienced premonitions, or warning dreams, about the disaster. Some of the accounts bore a remarkable similarity to the actual events.

wreck of the *Titanic*, author Morgan Robertson published a short novel called *Futility*. The story was about the wreck of a giant ship named the *Titan*; Robertson later claimed the entire plot for the story came to him while he was in a dreamlike trance.

The similarities between the *Titanic* and the fictional *Titan* seem uncanny. In Robertson's story the *Titan* was considered unsinkable. The ship was 800 feet (244m) long, had 24 lifeboats, carried 3,000 passengers, and sank in April after hitting an iceberg near midnight. The *Titan* was traveling at a speed of 25 knots (29 miles per hour or 46kph). The *Titanic* was also considered unsinkable. It was 882 feet (269m) long, had 24 lifeboats, carried about 2,200 passengers, and sank in April after hitting an iceberg near midnight. The *Titanic* was traveling at a speed of 23 knots (26 miles per hour or 42kph). There were other similarities as well: Both the *Titan* and *Titanic* hit icebergs on the starboard, or right, side; and both had too few lifeboats to save the number of passengers on board.

Robertson's book generated great interest after the *Titanic* disaster. In later printings it was renamed *The Wreck of the Titan*. Since that time, the story has been reprinted countless times, usually accompanied by claims that it was a result of precognitive dreaming. Even skeptics admit to eerie similarities between the real and fictional shipwrecks. However, most doubt the parallels are related to extrasensory perception.

Skeptics explain that Robertson was simply a good storyteller. Although no luxury liners as big as the *Titanic* had yet to be constructed, Robertson could easily have imagined a ship of that size. Also, many disasters in previous years had involved ships hitting icebergs and sinking in the North Atlantic. A majority of the wrecks occurred in April when warmer weather melted polar ice and created icebergs.

Did You Know?

An average person has up to a dozen dreams a night, most of which are instantly forgotten.

Robertson could have made educated guesses about the future and constructed a disaster story around his research. The basic technical concepts might have even come to him in a dream. Or the similarities between the real and fictional disasters might just have been coincidence. Gardner uses the term "probable improbability" to describe the idea that Robertson devised the precognitive plot of his story by chance:

> When thousands of stories are published about imaginary disasters—earthquakes, fires, floods, great battles, volcanic eruptions, tragic wrecks on land and sea and in the air—is it not likely that *some* will display astonishing parallels with actual disasters to come? Robertson's novel happens to be the best example we know of a "probable improbability" within the enormously large . . . universe of fictional possibilities.[49]

Group Premonitions

Whatever Gardner's analysis, a number of people had precognitive dreams about the wreck of the *Titanic*. When the same vision of the future is experienced by a large group of people, it is called a group premonition. One of the most studied cases of a group premonition concerns a tragedy that occurred in 1966 in the little mining town of Aberfan, Wales.

Coal mining companies had been extracting coal from Merthyr Mountain, directly above Aberfan, since the 1910s. As part of the mining process, tons of loose rock that had been separated from the coal was piled above the town. For nearly 50 years, the 1,000 people living in Aberfan worried that the coal waste might someday come crashing down on their town.

At 9:15 a.m. on October 21, 1966, after two days of heavy rain, the worst nightmares of the villagers came true. A half-million tons of coal waste slid down in an avalanche and came to rest on the town's elementary school, which was buried under 39 feet (12m) of loose rock. Twenty-eight adults and 116 children between the ages of 7 and 10 were killed.

After the Aberfan disaster, a number of people reported having had precognitive dreams about the tragedy. According to paranormal investigator Preston E. Dennett:

> One lady had a nightmare that she suffocated in "deep blackness." Another dreamed of a small child being buried by a large landslide. Another clearly saw a schoolhouse be buried by an avalanche of coal, and rescue workers digging frantically for survivors. Another woke up from a nightmare in which she was being buried alive.
>
> . . . Probably the clearest of the premonitions was reported by a man in northwestern England who claimed that the night before the disaster, he had a dream which consisted only of letters being spelled out in dazzling light, A-B-E-R-F-A-N. At the time, the dream had no meaning to him. Hours later, he would realize with horror what it meant.[50]

Another chilling precognitive dream about Aberfan was reported by the mother of Eryl Mai Jones, one of the students at the school. The night before the disaster, the 9-year-old Eryl told her mother: "I dreamed I went to school and there was no school there. Something black had come down all over it."[51] Jones's mother doubtlessly dismissed the dream. People in Aberfan had been having such terrible nightmares for decades. However, this dream came true. Eryl was one of the victims of the rock slide.

Preventing Further Disasters

The Aberfan disaster, which killed about half of the students in the school, generated intense sadness throughout Great Britain. London psychiatrist J.C. Barker visited Aberfan the day after the disaster and was appalled by the devastation and suffering. Barker later wrote, "It then occurred to me that there might have been people, not necessarily in the Aberfan area, but possibly throughout Britain, who had experienced some forewarning of the disaster. . . . Since the Aberfan disaster was such an unusual one, I considered that it would provide an excellent opportunity to investigate precognition."[52]

Barker launched his investigation of precognition through an ad in the London *Evening Standard*. He requested that people contact him if they had premonitions about Aberfan. The story was picked up by newspapers all over Great Britain, and within a few weeks Barker received 200 replies. He felt that 60 letters warranted follow-up. After further study, Barker concluded that 35 people had precognitive dreams about the Aberfan coal pile avalanche.

Barker was fascinated by the data and believed it could be useful in saving lives. In an article about his research, Barker writes, "The time had surely come to call a halt to attempts to prove or disprove precognition. We should instead set about trying to harness and utilize it with a view to preventing further disasters."[53] The following year, Barker founded the British Premonitions Bureau (BPB) as a place where people could leave an official record of their precognitive dreams. In order to publicize the bureau, Barker ran periodic ads in newspapers, radio, and television.

The BPB opened its doors in early 1967, and during its first year the bureau received 500 letters describing precognitive dreams or premonitions, an average of 10 a week. (The bureau did not keep track of precognitive dreams of a personal nature, only those concerning events that might make headlines.) Most reports contained descriptions of car and train wrecks, airplane crashes, fires, political assassinations, and natural disasters.

The BPB was active for six years and received about 500 reports annually. While sifting through this large pile of precognitive dreams, premonitions, and hunches, Barker never received a flood of reports about an impending tragedy before it happened. Because significant cases were far fewer than expected, the BPB shut its doors in 1973.

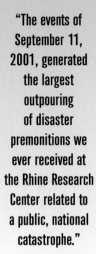

Dreams of 9/11

In the United States, the Rhine Research Center had amassed thousands of accounts of precognitive dreams since the early 1940s. Dozens of these dreams were said to have come true, including those concerning one of the most publicized disasters of the twenty-first century. According to Sally Rhine Feather, "The events of September 11, 2001, generated the largest outpouring of disaster premonitions we ever received at the Rhine Research Center related to a public, national catastrophe."[54]

The second hijacked airliner is seen moments before it strikes the second tower of the World Trade Center in New York City on September 11, 2001. ESP researchers say the terrorist attack generated a huge outpouring of people claiming to have had premonitions of the events of that day.

Feather compiled a list of 9/11 premonitions that included a woman named Marie who said she had a precognitive visual hallucination that the Pentagon was burning. It occurred two weeks before terrorists flew a jet into the building. In England a crime scene investigator named Guy Ottaway contacted Feather by e-mail shortly after the attack on the World Trade Center. He described a dream in which he saw an airplane heading toward a tall building and fire and plumes of smoke rising out of the top of the building.

In addition to specific dreams concerning the disaster, a number of people claimed they had precognitive dreams that caused them to change their travel plans on September 11, 2001. These people said that they survived because they did not get on the doomed flights that day. While no one knows the exact number of cancelations due to precognition, some have promoted a theory that the four jets that crashed that day had higher than normal vacancy rates due to premonitions. For example, American Airlines Flight 77, which hit the Pentagon, could have carried 289 people but only 64 seats were occupied, a 78 percent vacancy rate. American Airlines Flight 11, which crashed into the North Tower of the World Trade Center could have carried 351 passengers but only held 92, a 74 percent vacancy rate. Figures are similar for the other two planes involved in the 9/11 terrorist tragedy. Believers say these high vacancy rates are unusual when compared with the same flights a few days before September 11.

War, Pestilence, and Deprivation

More than a decade after the 9/11 attacks, dozens of websites continue to list precognitive dreams and premonitions concerning the event. And the disaster seems to have increased the number of people dreaming about upcoming terrorist attacks. Many descriptions of these precognitive dreams can be found on the Psychic Predictions Registry website, hosted by the Central Premonitions Registry (CPR), which began recording precognitive dreams and premonitions in 1968.

Listings on the Psychic Predictions website go back to 2002 and include many dire predictions which never came true. For

"Disaster!"

The terrorist attacks of September 11, 2001, were ostensibly foretold in a number of precognitive dreams. A 41-year-old English crime scene investigator named Guy Ottaway describes a dream he said he had several days before the attack:

> I was in a city, looking up. The main image I saw in my dream was two tall plumes of smoke. I saw fire, and I felt as though I was underneath the fallout from a volcano. I was taking cover under some kind of shelter from the rubble and boulders were flying through the air and raining down. I saw aircraft, and an image of my brother, a former pilot. I awoke in a cold sweat, feeling emotions of extreme fear and shock. . . . [I] wrote down the details of my premonition on a sheet of paper. The word I used in my notes to sum up the overall feeling was "Disaster!" I locked the notes in my drawer, and told two friends what I had dreamed.

Quoted in Sally Rhine Feather and Michael Schmicker, *The Gift*. New York: St. Martin's, 2005, p. 168.

example, in a posting from 2004 an anonymous contributor writes, "By the year 2012 . . . earth changes will have taken place. 1/3 of the world population will perish through war, pestilence, and deprivation. A new species of man will arise."[55] In more recent years, people claim to have dreamed that California would secede from the United States, World War III would begin, and the entire state of Arizona would experience a massive flood and remain underwater. Other scenarios described on the site as precognitive dreams involve terrorism, presidential assassination, massive hurricanes and earthquakes, and plane crashes.

The Boundaries of the Imagination

Those who believe in precognition think that something as extremely personal as a dream can predict events in the wider world. Skeptics say dreams are only mental movies made up of the thousands of thoughts that bombard the brain on a daily basis. All that is known for certain is that people spend about one-third of their lives asleep and one-fifth of that time dreaming. This means a person who is 30 years old has spent 10 years of his or her life asleep—and 2 complete years in dreamland. In dreams, time does not seem to exist, and the past, present, and future are seen as one. Dreamers are unleashed from their earthly bonds, and reality is only restricted by the boundaries of the imagination. In this state it might be entirely possible for the dreamer to see the improbable, accomplish the impossible, and, sometimes, understand the imponderable future.

NOTES

Chapter 1: Investigating ESP

1. Mark Twain, "Mental Telegraphy," *Harper's*, December 1891. http://harpers.org.
2. Twain, "Mental Telegraphy."
3. Quoted in Rosalind Heywood, *Beyond the Reach of Sense*. New York: E.P. Dutton, 1961, p. 38.
4. Heywood, *Beyond the Reach of Sense*, p. 43.
5. Quoted in Edmund Gurney et al., *Proceedings of the Society of Psychical Research*, vol. 1. London: Trubner, 1883, p. 147.
6. Quoted in Gurney et al., *Proceedings*, p. 43.
7. Gurney, Barrett, et al., *Proceedings*, p. 27.
8. Quoted in Edmund Gurney et al., *Phantasms of the Living*, vol. 1. London: Trubner, 1886, p. 194.
9. Joseph Banks Rhine, *New World of the Mind*. New York: William Sloan Associates, 1953, pp. 14–15.
10. Joseph Banks Rhine, *Extra-Sensory Perception*. Boston: Branden, 1997, p. 218.
11. Dean Radin, *Entangled Minds*. New York: Paraview, 2006, p. 88.
12. Fia Backström and Edgar Mitchell, "Private Lunar ESP: An Interview with Edgar Mitchell," *Cabinet*, Winter 2001/2002. www.cabinetmagazine.org.
13. Quoted in Benedict Carey, "Journal's Paper on ESP Expected to Prompt Outrage," *New York Times*, January 5, 2011. www.nytimes.com.

Chapter 2: Clairvoyance and the Senses

14. Diane Hennacy Powell, *The ESP Enigma*. New York: Walker, 2009, p. 59.
15. Quoted in Art History Archive, "The Origins of Surrealism." www.arthistoryarchive.com.
16. Quoted in Henry Hollen, *Clairaudient Transmission*. Hollywood, CA: Keats, 1931, p. 2.
17. Hollen, *Clairaudient Transmission*, p. 40.
18. Hollen, *Clairaudient Transmission*, p. 37.
19. Hollen, *Clairaudient Transmission*, p. 63.
20. Noreen Renier, *A Mind for Murder*. Charlottesville, VA: Hampton Roads, 2008, pp. 237–38.
21. Quoted in David Wright, "Psychic Bombshell in Laci Peterson Murder," Noreen Renier, April 29, 2003. http://noreenrenier.com.
22. Quoted in Wright, "Psychic Bombshell in Laci Peterson Murder."
23. Quoted in Douane D. James, "A Psychic Sleuth," Noreen Renier, April 29, 2003. http://noreenrenier.com.
24. Sally Rhine Feather and Michael Schmicker, *The Gift*. New York: St. Martin's, 2005, pp. 217–18.
25. Quoted in John Blake, "Do Loved Ones Bid Farewell from Beyond the Grave?" CNN, September 23, 2011. www.cnn.com.
26. Astoria Brown, "Clairalience," 2012. www.astoriabrown.com.
27. Feather and Schmicker, *The Gift*, p. 23.

Chapter 3: Extrasensory Warfare

28. Quoted in Ron McRae, *Mind Wars*. New York: St. Martin's, 1984, p. 32.
29. Quoted in Tim Rifat, "Lucid Viewing: The Way Forward in Remote Viewing," Biblioteca Pleyades, 2010. www.bibliotecapleyades.net.
30. Quoted in McRae, *Mind Wars*, p. 33.
31. Quoted in David G. Guyatt, "Toward a Psycho-Civilized Society," Biblioteca Pleyades, 2011. www.bibliotecapleyades.net.
32. Quoted in McRae, *Mind Wars*, p. 56.
33. Quoted in "What If Pat Price Were Here?," Heretical Notions, December 13, 2010. http://hereticalnotions.com.
34. Quoted in McRae, *Mind Wars*, p. 52.
35. Quoted in McRae, *Mind Wars*, p. 106.
36. Quoted in David Morehouse, *Psychic Warrior*. New York: St. Martin's, 1996, p. 54.
37. Morehouse, *Psychic Warrior*, p. 111.
38. Morehouse, *Psychic Warrior*, p. 111.
39. Jon Ronson, *The Men Who Stare at Goats*. New York: Simon & Schuster, 2004, p. 21.

Chapter 4: Dreaming of the Future

40. John William Dunne, *An Experiment with Time*. London: Purnell & Sons, 1948, p. 42.
41. Dunne, *An Experiment with Time*, p. 43.
42. Quoted in Dunne, *An Experiment with Time*, p. 43.
43. Dunne, *An Experiment with Time*, p. 59.
44. Martin Gardner, ed., *The Wreck of the Titanic Foretold?* Buffalo, NY: Prometheus, 1986, p. 8.
45. Quoted in David Gallup, *Aristotle on Sleep and Dreams*. Warminster, UK: Aris & Phillips, 1996, p. 111.
46. Ward Hill Lamon, *Recollections of Abraham Lincoln, 1847–1865*. Chicago: A.C. McClurg, 1895, pp. 116–17.
47. Quoted in Gardner, *The Wreck of the Titanic Foretold?*, p. 17.
48. Gardner, *The Wreck of the Titanic Foretold?*, p. 18.
49. Gardner, *The Wreck of the Titanic Foretold?*, pp. 35–36.
50. Preston E. Dennett, "Premonitions of Disaster," *Atlantis Rising Magazine*, 2012. www.atlantisrising.com.
51. Quoted in Stuart Holroyd, *Dream Worlds*. Garden City, NY: Doubleday, 1976, pp. 112–13.
52. Quoted in Andrew MacKenzie, *Riddle of the Future*. New York: Taplinger, 1974, p. 140.
53. Quoted in Dennett, "Premonitions of Disaster."
54. Feather and Schmicker, *The Gift*, p. 165.
55. Prophecies, "Old Site Predictions," 2012. http://prophecies.us.

For Further Research

Books

Faye Aldridge, *Real Messages From Heaven, and Other True Stories of Miracles, Divine Intervention and Supernatural Occurrences.* Shippensburg, PA: Destiny Image, 2011.

Jeff Belanger, *Paranormal Encounters: A Look at the Evidence.* New York: Rosen, 2011.

Arlene Billings and Beryl Dhanjal, *Supernatural Signs, Symbols, and Codes.* New York: Rosen, 2011.

Carl R. Green and William R. Sanford, *Amazing Out-of-Body Experiences.* Berkeley Heights, NJ: Enslow, 2011.

Rosemary Ellen Guiley, *Spirit Communications.* New York: Chelsea House, 2009.

Patricia D. Netzley, *Paranormal Activity.* San Diego: ReferencePoint, 2011.

Websites

Committee for Skeptical Inquiry (www.csicop.org). The Committee for Skeptical Inquiry promotes scientific inquiry, critical investigation, and the use of reason when examining controversial claims such as the existence of ESP and UFOs. The committee's journal, *Skeptical Inquirer*, is available on its website along with blogs, forums, and links related to disproving claims of paranormal events.

James Randi Educational Foundation (JREF) (www.randi.org). The JREF was founded in 1996 by stage magician James Randi to disprove claims of paranormal phenomena. The organization offers $1 million to anyone who can produce evidence of paranormal abilities under controlled conditions. The JREF website offers articles, blogs, digital media, and forums that challenge many paranormal claims.

Prophecies (http://prophecies.us). This website allows users to post the premonitions they receive during dreams or other telepathic experiences. These unedited posts include forecasts concerning politics, natural disasters, and even the winners of sporting events and reality TV shows. While most predictions are wrong, the descriptions of dreams and premonitions can be fascinating.

PSI Arcade (www.psiarcade.com). This website, hosted by the Noetic Institute, features online games created by parapsychologist Dean Radin. The games allow participants to test their telepathy, psychic abilities, intuition, and long-distance healing abilities.

Rhine Research Center (www.rhine.org). The center, founded by Joseph Banks Rhine and Louisa Rhine, has collected thousands of stories concerning premonitions, precognitive dreams, and other ESP phenomena. The website features blogs, interviews, and articles on the latest research into psi.

Society for Psychical Research (SPR) (www.spr.ac.uk). Founded in 1882, the society was the first to conduct scientific research concerning claims of ESP, ghosts, and other paranormal phenomena. Today the SPR continues its work, using this website in the digital world to promote and support psychical research with articles, events, and a forum for users to record their paranormal experiences.

STARstream Research (www.starpod.org). STARstream Research uses remote viewers to predict future security and risk developments in national and international affairs. The website features articles, blogs, videos, and other information concerning remote viewing, ESP, UFOs, and other shadowy psi operations allegedly undertaken by government agencies.

INDEX

Note: Page numbers in boldface indicate illustrations

L

M

N

O

P

S

T

U

Picture Credits

Cover: Thinkstock/Photodisc

AP Images: 69

© Bettmann/Corbis: 25, 57, 74

© Corbis: 50

iStockphoto: 33

© Masatomo Kuriya/Corbis: 80

© Amos Nachoum: 63

©Bernd Obermann/Corbis: 8

The Palmist I, 1989 (oil on canvas), Jacklin, Bill (Contemporary Artist)/
    Private Collection/The Bridgeman Art Library: 17

Jeremy Walker/Science Photo Library: 27

© Reuters/Corbis: 42

ABOUT THE AUTHOR

Stuart A. Kallen is the author of more than 250 nonfiction books for children and young adults. He has written on topics ranging from the theory of relativity to the history of rock and roll. In addition, Kallen has written award-winning children's videos and television scripts. In his spare time he is a singer/songwriter/guitarist in San Diego.